THE **WHO** OF WATFORD FC

Tales From The Vicarage

by John Murray

Tales From
www.talesfrom.com

John Mitchell:
All-time favourite
Watford FC player?
Wilf Rostron.

First published in Great Britain in 2018 by Tales From

© 2018 Tales From Ltd

Visual design, typography and photography by www.stonecreativedesign.com

Printed and bound by Page Bros Ltd

ISBN 978-1-912249-01-5

Tales From Ltd
107 Jupiter Drive, Hemel Hempstead, Herts HP2 5NU
Registered company number: 9082738
www.talesfrom.com
info@talesfrom.com

INTRODUCTION
BY JOHN MURRAY

As has so often been the case in the history of Watford Football Club, when it came to making this book, the fans played a pivotal part.

Putting together an A to Z of the Hornets was never going to be an easy task. And after some lengthy debates among the Tales From The Vicarage team, with seemingly no end to the stalemate, there was only one solution: ask the supporters to help get us over the line, just like they've done so many times on a Saturday afternoon.

And so a rallying call was issued to Watford fans on social media, seeking their suggestions for each letter – one per day over the final 26 days of the 2017/18 Premier League season.

From the letter 'A' on day one, the response was overwhelming, as social media served up a mixture of worthy contenders (Academy, Armstrong), unforgettable matches (Arsenal away, Anfield 1-0, "Almunia saves again") and dark humour (administration, Anglo-Italian Cup).

That pattern continued over the next four weeks as we took a joyous trip down memory lane and relived the history of the Hornets. Contributions flooded in every day, right up to Z-Cars, Zola-coaster and Luther Blissett's dog Ziggy for the last letter.

Then came the really hard part. Like a manager scratching his head over a teamsheet, we agonised about the final 26: Barnes or Blissett, Doyley or Deeney's goal, Wembley or Welbourne. Truth be told, we could have allocated every letter of the alphabet to Graham Taylor alone, such is his legacy at Vicarage Road.

The goal was to deliver a list that recognised the people, players and parts of the club that have made Watford what it is today – with plenty of memorable moments thrown in too. To keep things simple, it was decided that, for individuals, the letter would be for surnames, not first names (just in case anyone gets a shock when they turn to 'G'). We did allow one exception to this rule ... but 'Q' was never going to be easy!

Also included is a roll call of honourable mentions for many of the letters in yellow balls, giving a nod to club icons and identities not covered extensively elsewhere.

As with any book of this kind, the final selections are bound to stir up some debates, but it is a sign of the rich heritage of the club that almost every letter had no shortage of strong options.

An enormous thank you to the fans, and long may the list keep growing.

John Murray

TALES FROM THE VICARAGE

Connor Carpenter: Greatest ever Watford FC moment? *When we got promoted to the Premier League.*

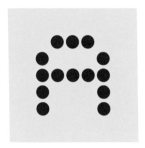

IS FOR...
ACADEMY

In the same year that Graham Taylor walked through the doors of Watford Football Club and started the fairytale journey that would take the team through all four divisions and into the elite of English football, another far less-heralded figure also joined the coaching staff. In many ways, though, his influence on the Hornets – both then and now – has been no less important.

With more than 200 games as a player for the club under his belt, Tom Walley was already well known to fans, but it's fair to say his work as Watford's youth team coach outshone anything he achieved in his playing career. Together with Taylor, the Welshman made the discovery and development of young players a priority and, day and night, would scout the country looking for potential stars to become part of the youth set-up.

Almen Abdi:
Swiss midfield maestro who was named player of the season in the spellbinding first year of the Pozzos' ownership.

Walley's tireless efforts and tough love approach soon produced impressive results, with Watford lifting the FA Youth Cup in 1982, beating Manchester United 7-6 on aggregate. And there was also a direct impact on the first team's fortunes throughout that decade, as a host of youngsters graduated to the seniors, including Kenny Jackett, John Barnes, Nigel Callaghan, Nigel Gibbs, David Holdsworth, Iwan Roberts, Darren Bazeley and David James.

The footballing side of things was by no means Walley's only focus. With Taylor determined to bring a family feel to Vicarage Road, Walley provided invaluable support to the young players off the field too, ensuring training wouldn't get in the way of their studies.

By the start of the 1990s, both men had left the club, but the factory line continued, with the likes of Richard Johnson and Tommy Smith a legacy of the work they had started. Then in 1998, the club launched its youth academy, which has unearthed a new treasure chest of stars. Ashley Young, Lloyd Doyley, Adrian Mariappa and Marvin Sordell were all graduates and, in March 2012, Britt Assombalonga became the 50th academy member to play for the first team. Each one is a product of the Hornets' proud tradition of producing and supporting their own players.

Gerry Armstrong: The Hornets' first ever goalscorer in the top division.

Walley's tireless efforts and tough love approach soon produced impressive results, with Watford lifting the FA Youth Cup in 1982, beating Manchester United 7-6 on aggregate

TALES FROM THE VICARAGE

THE A-Z OF WATFORD FC

Sarah Priestley:
Why Watford FC ?
*Born in Watford.
Love the
community of the
club and fans.*

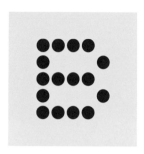

IS FOR...
BLISSETT

As the football world watched on in wonder at Watford's rise to the English game's top table in the 1980s, one player – Luther Blissett – was very much the face of the team's success.

❞ Luther was a trailblazer, a role model on and off the field, an inspiration to so many young Hornets ❞

Born in Jamaica in 1958, Luther Blissett moved to England aged six and soon graduated through the Hornets' youth teams. The teenager turned professional in 1975, and so began a love affair that saw him spend most of the next three decades at the club.

John Barnes: Wizardry winger and creator of so many of Blissett's goals.

Tommy Barnett: Inside forward and star of the 1930s who is second only to Blissett in Watford's all-time scoring list.

Forming a potent partnership up front with Ross Jenkins, Blissett played a pivotal role in the Hornets' surge from the Fourth Division. Athletic, strong and a natural finisher, he caused problems for defenders in all four tiers. Never more so than in Watford's first year in the top flight when he bagged 27 goals, more than anyone in the English Football League and any of Europe's elite divisions.

That led to a £1 million transfer to Italian giants AC Milan but, one year later, he was back at Vicarage Road, scoring 28 goals in all competitions. He netted three hat-tricks in all for the club and averaged 14 goals per season in the First Division.

Following a third brief stint at Watford in 1991, Blissett fulfilled several key roles on the sidelines in the 1990s – coach, assistant manager, reserve coach – as the club once again soared to the top flight.

The records for the Hornets roll off the tongue as quickly as he slotted in the goals in front of his adoring fans: all-time leading goalscorer (186); record games-holder (503); five-time top scorer; first senior England international in club history (scoring a hat-trick on his full debut). And then there were all the match-winning performances, be it four goals against Sunderland or the braces in cup wins at Old Trafford and Highbury.

Ian Bolton: Played in all four divisions and hailed by Graham Taylor as his best ever signing.

It came as no surprise when he became the first player to be inducted into Watford's Hall of Fame. Luther was a trailblazer, a role model on and off the field, an inspiration to so many young Hornets – which is why he was, and remains, the club's favourite son.

Aidy Boothroyd: The second manager to lead the club to the promised land of the Premier League.

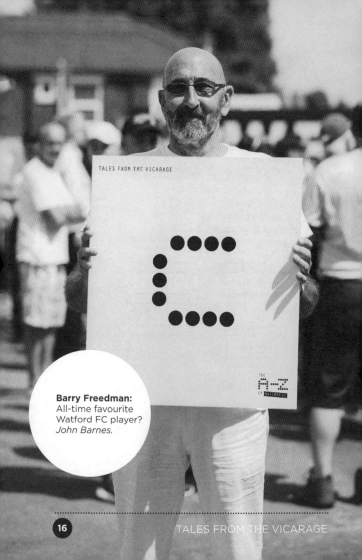

TALES FROM THE VICARAGE

Barry Freedman:
All-time favourite
Watford FC player?
John Barnes.

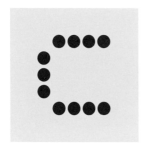

IS FOR...
COMMUNITY

The dynamic duo of Elton John and Graham Taylor didn't just transform Watford Football Club on the field, but off it too. From their arrival at Vicarage Road in the 1970s, the owner and manager set about creating a club that served and interacted with its community, where fans and locals felt they belonged. Watford became known as English football's family club.

As with so many things in his time at the Hornets, Taylor was the driving force. He would regularly seek the opinion of people on the streets and attend local events, and he made sure the players were part of the community too. The manager urged his squad to live no further than 30 miles from Vicarage Road and, over time, they even had to sign clauses in their contracts agreeing to appearances at local schools, work places and hospitals.

The sense of community also helped the club on the pitch – when visiting teams arrived at Vicarage Road they weren't just up against 11 opponents, but a whole town. Everyone was part of the journey up the Football League, including women and children.

At a time when the sport in England was blighted by hooliganism, Watford made going to the football a safe and enjoyable experience, becoming the first club in the land to create a family enclosure – at the front of the Main Stand. Taylor then raised £23,000 running the London Marathon in 1983 to help the enclosure be developed into the Family Terrace.

Marco Cassetti: Cool, classy Italian defender who epitomised Watford's transformation under Gianfranco Zola.

> **" Watford made going to the football a safe and enjoyable experience, becoming the first club in the land to create a family enclosure "**

Nigel Callaghan: A permanent fixture on the right wing in the 1980s who could cross with devastating accuracy.

A familiar figure on the terrace was Ann Swanson, who did so much in the community for the Hornets. In 1980, she launched the hugely successful Junior Hornets, bringing a whole new generation of fans into the club. Such was the impact of Watford's work that they won prestigious awards in 1984 and 1985 and were even praised in Parliament.

Today, the legacy continues through the club's Community Trust, which has reached more than 150,000 people, as well as the At Your Place events, where fans get exclusive access to players and staff. Watford's tradition of serving its community lives on.

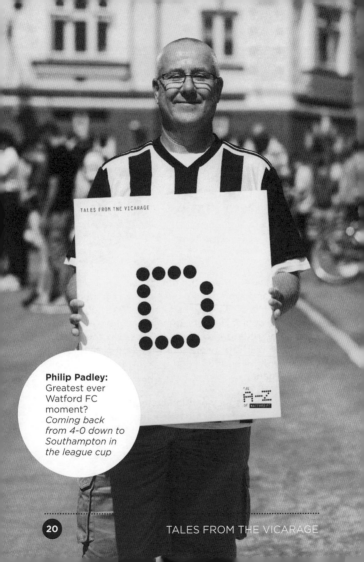

Philip Padley:
Greatest ever
Watford FC
moment?
*Coming back
from 4-0 down to
Southampton in
the league cup*

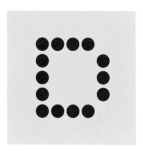

IS FOR...
DEENEY'S GOAL

Has there ever been a more glorious 19 seconds in Watford's history? It was the seventh minute of added time in the second leg of the 2013 Championship play-off semi-final between Watford and Leicester.

"From death's door, the Hornets had ripped off the hangman's noose and booked their place in the Wembley decider in the same time that it would take Usain Bolt to run 200m"

With the teams tied 2-2 on aggregate and extra time barely seconds away, the Hornets' dream of reaching the Premier League was suddenly in danger of becoming a nightmare as the Foxes won a controversial penalty. Anthony Knockaert flopped to the floor under a challenge from Marco Cassetti, referee Michael Oliver pointed to the spot, and a season that had brought so much excitement and ecstasy seemed set to end in the most miserable way.

Jay DeMerit: American defender who captained the club and memorably opened the scoring in the 2006 play-off final.

Luckily, goalkeeper Manuel Almunia had other ideas. The club captain leapt to his left to keep out Knockaert's penalty and start the most extraordinary sequence of events.

First, the Spanish stopper had to drag himself to his feet to deny Knockaert again from the rebound; then came a thumping clearance from Cassetti; the deftest of touches from Ikechi Anya and a dash forward; Fernando Forestieri's measured cross; Jonathan Hogg's selfless header; and Troy Deeney's net-bursting finish. From death's door, the Hornets had ripped off the hangman's noose and booked their place in the Wembley decider in the same time that it would take Usain Bolt to run 200m.

Cue pandemonium. Amid the carnage, you could see Deeney in the stands without his shirt, manager Gianfranco Zola falling over on the sidelines, and fans running deliriously all over the Vicarage Road pitch, with no specific destination in mind. For those watching at home, the intoxicating scenes were accompanied by the immortal words of Sky Sports commentator Bill Leslie: "Do not scratch your eyes."

Just a fortnight later, many of those same fans must have been sorely tempted to scratch their eyes for different reasons as Watford surrendered to Crystal Palace in the play-off final. Yet once the disappointment of missing out on the Premier League had subsided, nothing could ever take away the utter joy of those jaw-dropping final moments at Vicarage Road.

Lloyd Doyley:
Devoted servant who played more than 400 games across the defence over 15 years.

TALES FROM THE VICARAGE

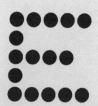

Alistair Nelson:
Whereabouts in
the Vicarage Road
stadium do you sit?
Family Stand.

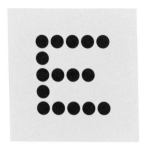

IS FOR...
EUROPE

Watford's first ever foray into European
football began on September 14 1983 at the
Betzenbergstadion in Germany. Qualification for
the UEFA Cup – the Europa League as it's known
today – was reward for their stunning effort to
finish runners-up behind Liverpool in the First
Division in 1982/83.

There was no group stage back then, with teams going straight into the knockout phase, and the Hornets' adventure was nearly over as quickly as it had begun; Jimmy Gilligan becoming the first Hornet to score in European competition was a rare highlight for the 2,000 travelling fans in a 3-1 first-leg defeat to Kaiserslautern.

Keith Eddy: Midfielder and key figure in the Third Division title-winning team of 1968/69 who played 200-plus games.

But on a famous night under the lights at Vicarage Road, Watford turned the tie on its head in a match that manager Graham Taylor described as "the greatest result of my career". Roared on by 21,457 frenzied fans, the Hornets were level within just seven minutes, thanks to an own goal and a strike from Ian Richardson. The teenager then netted again with a sliding volley in the second half to seal the club's first ever European victory.

The Hornets had to do it the hard way again in the second round. Few fancied their chances of progressing after they only managed a 1-1 draw at home to Levski Spartak. While the Bulgarians boasted six internationals, many of Taylor's charges were fresh out of the reserves that season, with the team's average age for the return leg just 21.

Barry Endean:
From pub team to prolific goalscorer, and like Eddy, a pivotal player in the promotion to the second tier.

The situation looked even bleaker in front of 60,000 home fans at the intimidating Vasil Levski National Stadium when Levski went ahead after three minutes, but an instant reply from Nigel Callaghan, and goals from captain Wilf Rostron and Richardson in extra time crowned another remarkable comeback.

A third-round clash with Sparta Prague, who had already knocked out Real Madrid, proved a step too far for the young Hornets. A 3-2 home defeat was followed by a 4-0 loss in Czechoslovakia, and the incredible UEFA Cup rollercoaster ride was over. It remains the club's only taste of European competition. For now …

John Eustace:
No-nonsense midfielder who wore the captain's armband with enormous pride.

" **On a famous night under the lights at Vicarage Road, Watford turned the tie on its head in a match that manager Graham Taylor described as "the greatest result of my career"** "

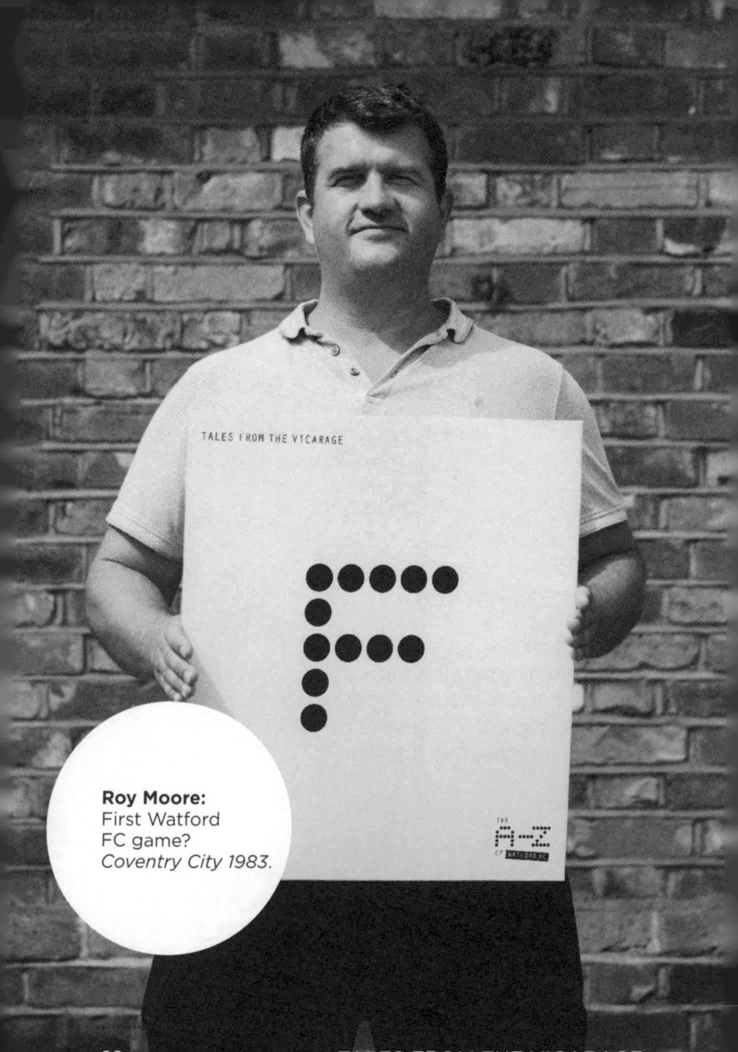

TALES FROM THE VICARAGE

F

Roy Moore:
First Watford
FC game?
Coventry City 1983.

THE A-Z
OF WATFORD FC

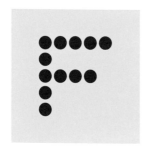

IS FOR...
FORMED IN 1881

For a club that is now accustomed to the glitz and glamour of the Premier League, Watford's formation was grounded in the humblest of beginnings.

" In those early days, the club had enough different names, grounds and kits to start a whole league of its own "

It all started back in 1881 when a group of young men from local Watford families began playing football at Cassiobury Park – the 19th-century equivalent of a bunch of lads having a kickabout. The leading figure was Henry Grover, who is credited as the founder of this new team – Watford Rovers – an amateur side that quickly replaced Hertfordshire Rangers as the town's No.1 club. According to Watford historian Trefor Jones, their first known game was a 2-0 win away to Nascot on January 21 1882.

In those early days, the club had enough different names, grounds and kits to start a whole league of its own. Wearing strips ranging from blue to stripes that covered most of the rainbow, the team played all around Watford, including Vicarage Meadow (near today's Vicarage Road stadium), Rose & Crown Meadow, and Colney Butts Meadow. In 1890, Watford Rovers settled at Cassio Road as part of the West Hertfordshire Sports Club, which led to a change of name three years later to West Hertfordshire.

From the Rookery End: Popular podcast produced by lifelong Watford fans.

Their first official competitive games took place in the 1886/87 season, including an FA Cup defeat to Swindon where Grover played in defence.

Cup success wasn't far away, though, with victory in the Herts County Cup final against familiar foe Hoddesdon in 1889. West Herts went on to join the Southern League Second Division in 1896 and started paying players in 1897.

Ken Furphy:
Manager who led the Hornets to the Second Division and FA Cup semi-final for the first time.

However, a year later, struggling to meet the demands of professional football, they merged with Watford St Mary's, and Watford Football Club was born. Within two seasons, Watford FC had won the Southern League Second Division and promotion to the First Division.

Paul Furlong:
Striker and player of the season whose goals led to a club-record transfer to Chelsea in 1994.

In 2013, a group of fans started the 1881 Movement, with the goal of improving the atmosphere and support at Vicarage Road. With their songs, flags and enormous banners, they are now a well-established presence in the Rookery End, while also a constant reminder of the year when it all began.

TALES FROM THE VICARAGE

Adam Godfrey:
Why Watford FC?
*My mum brought
me to my first
match and hooked
after that!*

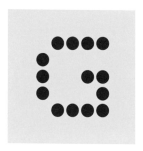

IS FOR...
GOODALL

In May 2018, a headstone was laid at an unmarked grave in Vicarage Road cemetery. The first line reads: "Here lies John Goodall 1863-1942." Installed by Watford FC, and adorned with the club's crescent, the new gravestone goes on to pay tribute to the extraordinary talents and achievements of the Hornets' first ever manager.

"Goodall brought instant success – and a big thumbs-up for Watford's decision to appoint a manager over 30 years after their formation"

Nigel Gibbs:
Right back who debuted in the UEFA Cup and went on to play 411 games.

The man known universally as 'Johnny Allgood' caused quite a stir when he joined Watford in 1903. He might not have had the flash cars or the eye-watering salary, but this was very much the Beckham or Ronaldo of Victorian football. He had top-scored for Preston in their 1888/89 double-winning season, led the forward line for Derby County for a decade – at the time one of the best teams in the land – and won 14 England caps. What's more, his talents were by no means restricted to football – he played first-class cricket and even competed for England at bowls.

As well as a superstar status, Goodall brought instant success – and a big thumbs-up for Watford's decision to appoint a manager over 30 years after their formation. His team was unbeaten in the 1903/04 season, notching an impressive 18 wins and two draws from 20 league games to ensure promotion to the Southern League First Division at the very first time of asking.

Not that the manager always had it all his own way. Before his appointment, Watford's starting XI for each match had always been chosen by the club's committee, and Johnny Allgood still had to run every teamsheet past the hierarchy for their approval.

Jimmy Gilligan:
First Hornet to score a goal in European competition and, at 18, the youngest goalscorer in the top flight.

It mattered not one bit. The club stayed in the Southern League's top division for Goodall's remaining six seasons in charge, with a best finish of ninth coming in 1907. And it wasn't just from the sidelines where he made a significant contribution. For the first four years of his tenure, he continued to lace up his boots at inside forward, and still holds the record for being Watford's oldest ever player at 44.

Ghost goal:
Infamous incident when referee Stuart Attwell awarded a goal to Reading after the ball had bobbled out for a corner.

TALES FROM THE VICARAGE

Hilda Hasley:
Greatest ever
Watford FC
moment?
*Winning Supporter
of the Year!*

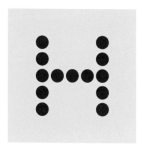

IS FOR...
HORNETS

In a football world rammed full of nicknames ranging from Toffees and Tractor Boys to Cobblers and the Cod Army, Watford will always hold a special place as the Hornets. Watford are the Hornets, the Hornets are Watford, with the club's yellow-and-black kit easily conjuring up images of Britain's biggest wasp.

It hasn't always been the case, though. Cast your mind back 100 years and the club didn't even have a nickname. It was only in the late 1910s, when Watford wore black-and-white stripes, that some supporters began referring to them as the Magpies – their very first nickname.

Harry the Hornet: Much-loved club mascot who had a memorable spat with Crystal Palace's Wilfried Zaha.

Just like the colours, though, the name didn't last long, and when Benskins Brewery bought the Vicarage Road stadium in 1921, Watford soon became known as the Brewers. Once again, it didn't prove a popular choice; in 1927, the club adopted a new blue-and-white kit, and the nickname quickly changed too – to the imaginatively named Blues!

So how did the Hornets come about? The answer, as is so often the case, is thanks to the fans. In 1959, Watford swapped their blue strip for gold and black. At the same time, the supporters were given the

With the fans showing far more creativity than previous offerings, Comets, Wasps and Tigers were all in the mix, but the winning choice was the Hornets

chance to suggest a new nickname in a club competition. With the fans showing far more creativity than previous offerings, Comets, Wasps and Tigers were all in the mix, but the winning choice was the Hornets.

Whether it was the new colours, the new nickname or the fact that Cliff Holton scored a club-record 48 goals in the 1959/60 season, the changes clearly had the desired effect. Watford instantly won promotion to the Third Division, with many of their victories accompanied by now-familiar newspaper headlines about a Hornets' sting in the tail.

Andy Hessenthaler: Midfielder and captain in the mid-1990s who boasted a tremendous work-rate.

A hornet badge soon followed, but this was replaced by a hart. The hart is a male deer that represents Hertfordshire, the county where for many decades Watford were the only Football League club. And while it remains the club's emblem today, Watford will always be identified as the Hornets, as reflected in the song that rings out every matchday: *Come on you 'Orns.*

Heidar Helguson: Icelandic forward and fan favourite who scored on debut against Liverpool.

TALES FROM THE VICARAGE

Neil Stevenson:
All-time favourite
Watford FC player?
Ian Bolton.

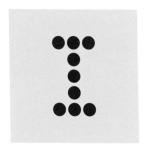

IS FOR...
I'M WATFORD TILL I DIE

For a team synonymous with one of the world's biggest music stars, it's fitting that Watford have a rich history of singing from the stands – and more songs than even Sir Elton John has released over the past half a century.

One chant has stood the test of time more than any other. Four decades on from when Elton took over his boyhood club, *Elton John's Taylor-Made Army* still booms around Vicarage Road and all over the country on Hornets' away days – paying tribute to the chairman and manager who revolutionised the club.

While most chants typically last a minute or two at best, Hornets fans have been known to sing this anthem for 10-20 minute spells, or even the best part of a half. The same lyrics, and same beat of the drum, again and again, a rallying call from the supporters urging the Hornets forward or to keep the opposition at bay. And when Elton and 'GT' returned in the mid-1990s, so did the song – and it's never gone away.

Other chants that can be regularly heard at Vicarage Road include *Yellow Army, Come on you 'Orns* whenever the team wins a corner, and an album's worth of songs directed at arch-rivals Luton Town (many of them unprintable in these pages!).

There are also plenty for individual players, often based on hits by the likes of Spandau Ballet, The Proclaimers and Billy Ray Cyrus – and used by supporters of clubs across the country, with a few different lyrics.

In recent years, the 1881 Movement singing section in the Rookery End has brought more chants, and a lot more volume, to Vicarage Road. There are few better sounds than hearing the whole crowd in unison, singing a tribute to Quique Sanchez Flores, or a song for Abdoulaye Doucouré – to the tune of Earth, Wind & Fire's *September*.

But there is nothing more spine-tingling than when the clock strikes the 72nd minute on a matchday at Vicarage Road. At that point, Hornets fans rise as one to sing *There's only one Graham Taylor,* who was 72 at the time of his sudden passing in January 2017.

Odion Ighalo:
The top scorer in England in 2015, his goals helped propel the Hornets to the Premier League.

" **Four decades on from when Elton took over his boyhood club, *Elton John's Taylor-Made Army* still booms around Vicarage Road and all over the country on Hornets' away days** "

TALES FROM THE VICARAGE

THE
A–Z
OF WATFORD FC

Nick Elton:
Whereabouts in
the Vicarage Road
stadium do you sit?
Elton John Stand.

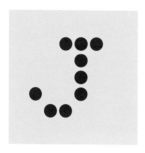

IS FOR...
JOHN

With his flamboyant dress sense, huge glasses and more hats than the Queen, Elton John was one of the world's biggest popstars when he replaced Jim Bonser to become the Hornets' chairman in 1976.

....

" Elton was a lifelong Hornet, who had first stood on the Vicarage Road terraces aged six and was prepared to invest the necessary funds and energy into the club to achieve his dream "

....

Watford had never known anything like it – particularly when the new owner declared his ambition to take the Fourth Division side into the top flight. Overly optimistic? Maybe, but Elton was a lifelong Hornet, who had first stood on the Vicarage Road terraces aged six and was prepared to invest the necessary funds and energy into the club to achieve his dream.

He soon made the best decision of his entire tenure when he persuaded Graham Taylor to leave Lincoln City, from the league above, and take the manager's job. The pair immediately clicked, with Elton regularly involved but happy to let his key staff manage affairs. He was determined to bring a family feel to the club too and forged strong relationships with the players, who called him Elton, or 'Mr Chairman' when appropriate. The friendly atmosphere even extended to the boardroom.

George James:
Forward from the 1930s with an extraordinary strike rate of 67 goals in 83 games.

Together, chairman and manager built a team that confounded all expectations, in record time, rising from the fourth tier to runners-up in the First Division in just six

seasons. The next year, a global audience watched Elton wipe away his tears at Wembley after the FA Cup final loss to Everton.

Ross Jenkins: Talismanic forward who played in all four divisions.

After selling the club in 1990, his return as chairman in 1997 meant the band was back together – Taylor as manager, and Luther Blissett and Kenny Jackett, fan favourites from the golden 1980s era, on the coaching staff. The good times rolled again, with back-to-back promotions from the Second Division to the Premier League.

Elton said goodbye again in 2002, but he has always remained a part of the club – be it his 'Buy back the Vic' concert at Vicarage Road in 2005 or becoming honorary life president. Most special of all, though, was the unveiling of the Sir Elton John Stand in 2014, an honour he described as "one of the greatest days of my life".

Slavisa Jokanovic: Led Watford to the Premier League in 2015, despite being the club's fourth manager of the season.

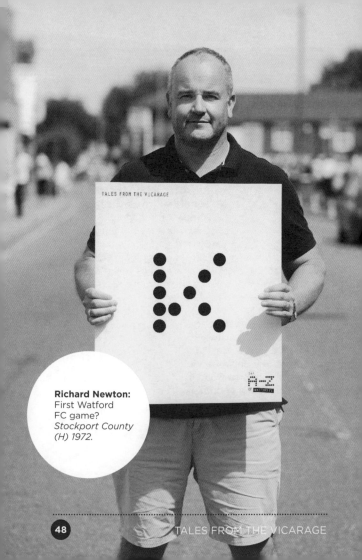

TALES FROM THE VICARAGE

Richard Newton:
First Watford
FC game?
*Stockport County
(H) 1972.*

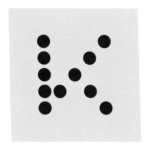

IS FOR...
KEEPERS

What is it about Watford and goalkeepers?
Flick through the chapters of the club's memorable
moments and the man between the sticks has
regularly been a central figure.

There's Steve Sherwood's controversial coming together with Andy Gray in the 1984 FA Cup final, Manuel Almunia's play-off penalty save in 2013, and even the shock call-up of the unknown Gary Plumley for the 1987 FA Cup semi-final.

Peter Kennedy: Wingback from Northern Ireland with a wicked left foot who played in the first team to reach the Premier League.

Perhaps it's no coincidence that some of the Hornets' finest players have also been keepers. Ever since Andy Rankin was named the first player of the season in 1973, goalkeepers have been regular recipients of the award – something that always concerned Graham Taylor, who preferred his best players to be scoring goals at the other end! In all, keepers have won the prestigious prize 12 times, be it Kevin Miller's double in the 1990s or Heurelho Gomes in 2016.

Greatest of all was Tony Coton, who holds the honour of being the only Hornet to win the award three times. The Birmingham-born stopper may have conceded five goals on debut in 1984 but, by the time he waved farewell six years later, there was no doubting his talents. The fearless Coton was a wonderful shot-stopper and a great character on and off the field.

The roll call also includes: a young Pat Jennings, who won his first caps for Northern Ireland thanks to his form for the Hornets; Sherwood, who played in all four tiers as Watford climbed the football pyramid; David James, player of the year at just 20 before being snapped up by Liverpool; and Ben Foster, the Manchester United loanee who became one of our own as he starred in Aidy Boothroyd's promotion-winning campaign, and then returned to Vicarage Road in 2018.

For longevity, though, no one can beat Alec Chamberlain, who spent 21 years at the club as a player and coach, played in three divisions, won three promotions, and made his final Premier League appearance aged 42. He also achieved the rarest of feats for a Hornet – becoming a fan favourite despite having previously played for arch-rivals Luton.

Harry Kent: Long-serving manager who led the club to the Southern League First Division title in 1915.

" Coton may have conceded five goals on debut in 1984 but, by the time he waved farewell six years later, there was no doubting his talents "

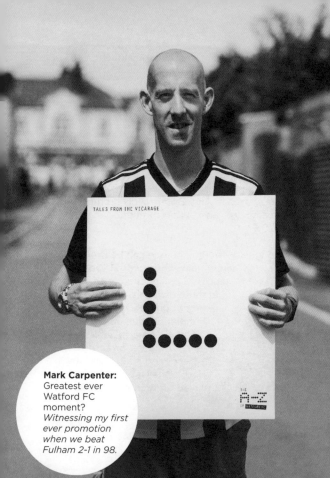

TALES FROM THE VICARAGE

Mark Carpenter:
Greatest ever
Watford FC
moment?
*Witnessing my first
ever promotion
when we beat
Fulham 2-1 in 98.*

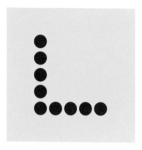

IS FOR...
L***N TOWN

We know what you're thinking - have they really given a letter to our bitter rivals in a book all about Watford? To many Hornets, any reference whatsoever to the old enemy is hard to stomach - some even find it hard to utter their name, preferring "Them lot up the M1" or other less polite references!

But truth be told, Luton Town – there you go, we've said it – are an integral part of Watford's history and identity. The Hornets might currently be looking down on their rivals from their Premier League perch, but – separated by just 17 miles and the Hertfordshire/Bedfordshire border – the two teams have been close together throughout much of their footballing lives. Too close for comfort at times.

You have to go back to October 29 1898 for their first meeting in the FA Cup third qualifying round. In a sign of things to come, they were inseparable, with a replay required before Luton emerged victorious. The rivalry gradually grew in the 1920s and '30s in the Third Division South, including the 1921 clash that drew a record crowd of almost 13,000 at Cassio Road. After a hiatus of nearly 30 years, they were reunited in the Third Division in the 1960s and again in the Second Division the following decade.

Ray Lewington: Manager who kept the club in the second tier and reached two cup semi-finals at a very challenging time.

However, it was in the 1980s – when both clubs won promotion to the top flight and were in the national spotlight – that things became really heated. Never more so than the league match at Kenilworth Road in 1984. Of far more significance

"The two teams have been close together throughout much of their footballing lives. Too close for comfort at times"

than the Hornets' 2-1 win was the red card for skipper Wilf Rostron that ruled him out of the FA Cup final; no surprises for guessing who got the blame!

Many more tense battles ensued as the clubs went up and down the divisions together, but one match stands head and shoulders above all others. After 10 years without a win, Watford thrashed Luton 4-0 on their own turf – all four goals coming in the first 29 minutes – on their way to promotion from the Second Division. It was certainly worth the wait.

Jan Lohman: Dutchman who became the first non-British player to join the Hornets from an overseas club

TALES FROM THE VICARAGE

THE
A–Z
OF WATFORD FC

Martin Rayment:
All-time favourite
Watford FC player?
Luther.

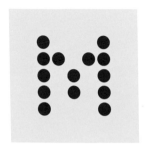

IS FOR...
MILLENNIUM STADIUM

The Welsh capital might not be an obvious location for one of the most famous days in Watford's history but, with Wembley under construction, it fell to the Millennium Stadium to host the 2006 Championship play-off final between the Hornets and Leeds United.

"Watford have enjoyed, and suffered, the full range of emotions in the play-offs over the years"

After tearing up pre-season predictions to finish third in the table, Aidy Boothroyd's team strolled into the decider with a 3-0 aggregate semi-final win over Crystal Palace and, bursting with confidence in Cardiff, they then proceeded to chalk up the same scoreline against Leeds. A header from captain Jay DeMerit and a Darius Henderson penalty, sandwiched between an own goal, ensured Boothroyd would become just the second manager to lead Watford into the Premier League.

Such was their self-belief that the players have since insisted the match was won before they even set foot on the pitch. It had become a habit for the Hornets to make plenty of noise in the tunnel pre-match, shouting, slapping and geeing each other up – and one look across at their subdued opponents was all it took to convince them that they would triumph.

Watford have enjoyed, and suffered, the full range of emotions in the play-offs over the years, with Boothroyd experiencing the other end of the spectrum two seasons later in a 6-1 aggregate semi-final defeat to Hull City. There was a similar outcome, albeit

Aidy Mariappa: Defender who came through the youth system to star at the highest level in two spells at the club.

a lot closer, in the club's first play-off appearance in 1989 when Steve Harrison's men lost to Blackburn Rovers on away goals. Then in 2013 came the ecstasy of Troy Deeney's late winner against Leicester followed by the agony of defeat to Crystal Palace in the final.

Tommy Mooney: Iconic striker who was a central figure in the promotion-winning teams of the late 1990s.

No such woes in 1999, however. After Graham Taylor's side snuck into the play-offs thanks to a Tommy Mooney-inspired seven wins from their last eight games, the semi-final against Birmingham was decided by a penalty shootout, with goalkeeper Alec Chamberlain the hero in a nailbiting 7-6 win at St Andrew's.

Goalscorers Nick Wright and Allan Smart then wrote their names into club folklore in the final against Bolton at Wembley as Watford reached the Premier League for the first time.

John McClelland: Ultra-dependable defender twice voted player of the season who represented Northern Ireland at the World Cup.

TALES FROM THE VICARAGE

Wayne Godfrey:
Greatest ever
Watford FC
moment?
*Watford 7
Southampton 1.*

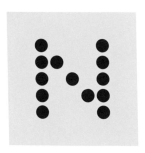

IS FOR...
NATIONAL SERVICE

When Gerry Armstrong headed home against
Honduras at the 1982 World Cup, it was greeted with
celebrations all over Northern Ireland – and in many
Watford living rooms too.

" Taking on Brazil in the Maracana, the Watford winger gave his own demonstration of the beautiful game, weaving past five opponents before finishing with his right foot "

After making history as the club's first ever goalscorer in the First Division the previous year, the Belfast man had just become the first Hornets player to score in the biggest football tournament on the planet. And he gave Watford fans plenty more reasons to be proud that summer, scoring three goals in all, including the winner against hosts Spain.

Over the years, some of the finest players to don a Watford shirt have graced the international stage – from Algeria and Australia to Switzerland and South Korea, with Mexico, Morocco and many more in between. But while it is a regular sight today to see the squad represent their countries around the world, it was a much rarer occurrence in the pre-Premier League era.

In 1982, Luther Blissett became the Hornets' first full England international, as well as the first black player to score for the Three Lions, when he netted a hat-trick against Luxembourg. John Barnes's

first England goal two years later was even more memorable. Taking on Brazil in the Maracana, the Watford winger gave his own demonstration of the beautiful game, weaving past five opponents before finishing with his right foot.

With 31 England appearances during his time at Vicarage Road, Barnes remains the most capped Watford player– alongside Kenny Jackett, the versatile left-sided player who spent his whole career at Watford and won 31 caps for Wales. Other prominent internationals from their time at Watford include: Heidar Helguson (Iceland, 28 caps); former captains Jay DeMerit (USA, 23 caps) and Robert Page (Wales, 21 caps); and John McClelland (Northern Ireland, 20 caps).

Gifton Noel-Williams: Wonderfully talented striker who became the Hornets' youngest ever goalscorer at just 16.

Turn back the clock a century, and Watford players were giving a very different kind of national service. Twelve players served their country in World War One; the club paid a special tribute to them during the 2014/15 season with a black-and-white striped away kit – the same colours the team wore throughout the Great War.

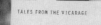

TALES FROM THE VICARAGE

Robin Lingwood:
Why Watford FC?
*My closest league
club as a kid.*

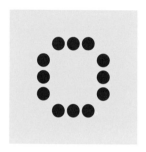

IS FOR...
OCCUPATION ROAD

From top to bottom, it spans just 500m but, for
Watford fans, it might just be the most important
road in the whole town. Occupation Road is
an iconic path that has been well trodden by
generations of Hornets, whether heading down the
hill to the match from Vicarage Road or walking up
from Cardiff Road.

This special stretch of road runs parallel to the Sir Elton John Stand and is the gateway to the stadium's heartbeat – the Rookery End, the main stand for home supporters.

Whatever your age, whatever your experiences as a Hornet, Occupation Road cannot fail to conjure up some strong sensations and memories: the anticipation and buzz before kick-off; watching the team arrive; the smell of burgers and onions piercing your nostrils; walking past the away fans; grabbing an autograph at the 'Players and match officials' entrance; shovelling snow to help make sure the game will go ahead; cutting through the neighbouring gardens to beat the crowds; programme sellers; Harry's 50/50; turnstiles; garages; queues for play-off final tickets; post-match euphoria or (plenty of) post-mortems.

To the north of the stadium, Vicarage Road itself has several notable landmarks, in addition to the collection of match-day stalls, eateries and pubs that provide supporters with welcome refreshments – or the chance to drown their sorrows. The Hornets Shop is packed full of customers every matchday and offers regular opportunities for supporters to meet the players. At Vicarage Road Cemetery, meanwhile, the club has its own memorial area.

October 4 1997:
The day when Watford thrashed Luton 4-0 at Kenilworth Road, after 10 years without a win.

For many years, the Farm Terrace allotments dominated the area of land to the south of the stadium. Dating back to 1882, the site was home to more than 100 individual allotments until 2017 when the plots were removed as part of the council's major regeneration scheme.

Over to the west, behind the Graham Taylor Stand, lies Watford General Hospital. Many a new Hornet has been born overlooking the famous ground and the iconic landmarks that are such a part of the club.

....

Whatever your age, whatever your experiences as a Hornet, Occupation Road cannot fail to conjure up some strong sensations and memories

....

TALES FROM THE VICARAGE

Taylor Knight:
All-time favourite Watford FC player?
Troy Deeney.

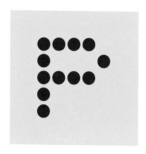

IS FOR...
POZZO

The summer of 2012 changed the face of Watford FC as we knew it. On June 29, the club announced it had been bought by the Pozzo family – namely, Gianpaolo and his son Gino, owners of Udinese and Granada. To Hornets fans, this offered the tantalising prospect of stability, success and maybe even silverware.

Gianpaolo, an Italian businessman, had transformed the fortunes of Serie A side Udinese since buying the club in 1986. Granada were next to benefit from the magic touch, becoming a regular presence in Spain's Primera Liga until a change of ownership in 2016.

Come 2012, Gianpaolo had handed the reins of the family football operations to Gino, and the younger Pozzo became Watford's owner. One of his first acts was to renovate the stadium, which led to the Sir Elton John Stand opening in 2014. Most excitingly, the Pozzos brought a worldwide scouting network to Vicarage Road, famed for discovering young talent in all corners of the globe. They also boasted an impressive track record of selling these players for considerable profits. Take Alexis Sanchez, signed for less than £1 million, sold to Barcelona for £23 million five years later.

Watford instantly benefited from the Pozzos' scouting and multi-ownership, with a host of exotic names flooding into the club alongside manager Gianfranco Zola that summer. Matej Vydra, Almen Abdi, Marco Cassetti, Fernando

Gary Porter: Left-footed midfielder and dead-ball expert who appeared more than 400 times for the Hornets.

Forestieri and Joel Ekstrand were just a handful of the overseas loanees who joined from Udinese and Granada.

Robert Page: Welsh international who captained Watford's successive promotion-winning sides at the end of the 1990s.

Rival clubs were soon grumbling about this so-called loophole that the Hornets had exploited. Not that anyone at the club cared – the Hornets conjured up some of their most exciting football in living memory, coming within a play-off final of reaching the Premier League at the Pozzos' first attempt.

They didn't have to wait long, though – two years later, under the shrewd guidance of manager Slavisa Jokanovic, Watford finished second in the Championship to win promotion to the top flight. Project Pozzo had taken off.

Kevin Phillips: Small striker who made a huge impact in three seasons, averaging almost a goal every other game.

The Pozzos brought a worldwide scouting network to Vicarage Road, famed for discovering young talent in all corners of the globe

TALES FROM THE VICARAGE

Ian Wooding:
Whereabouts in
the Vicarage Road
stadium do you sit?
The Rookery End.

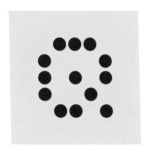

IS FOR...
QUIQUE SANCHEZ FLORES

Watford's new manager for the 2015/16 season
faced a daunting task. If Quique Sanchez Flores
was to keep the newly promoted club in the
Premier League, he would have to confound history
as well as the pre-season predictions of pretty
much every pundit – while integrating 15 new faces
into his squad.

> **Flores was a popular figure around the club and with the wider football public, prompting the BBC's Ian Wright to crown him the "new sheriff in town"**

Yet come May 2016, the Hornets were sitting pretty in 13th place and the Spaniard had achieved something that neither Graham Taylor nor Aidy Boothroyd could manage – becoming the first man to keep Watford in the Premier League.

And the Hornets had done it in style, which was entirely appropriate for a manager who brought a suave sophistication to Vicarage Road. Friendly and approachable, with good looks and a dress sense to match, Flores was a popular figure around the club and with the wider football public, prompting the BBC's Ian Wright to crown him the "new sheriff in town".

Capped 15 times for Spain at right-back, he boasted a rich heritage of football (his father played for Real Madrid) and culture (his mother was an actress and singer, while his aunt was the most

famous flamenco dancer in Spain). He also had managerial pedigree, having won the Europa League with Atletico Madrid and taken Valencia into the Champions League.

That talent was soon evident. A win over Swansea in September started the Hornets' ignition and, as belief grew, victories followed over Newcastle, Stoke and West Ham. It got even better in December. A glorious 3-0 defeat of Liverpool – their fourth win in a row – moved Watford to within a point of the Champions League places at Christmas, and led to Flores and striker Odion Ighalo winning the Premier League manager and player of the month awards.

While the league form tailed off in the New Year, Flores's side set out on a thrilling FA Cup run, which included a sensational quarter-final win at the Emirates Stadium over holders and favourites Arsenal, Adlene Guedioura's thunderbolt sending 9,000 travelling Hornets into delirium.

The journey ended in the semi-final at Wembley against Crystal Palace and, one month later, Flores had gone too, but he left behind fond memories and a proud chapter in Watford's history.

TALES FROM THE VICARAGE

Peter Ryan:
First Watford
FC game?
*Not sure, a
1960s friendly at
Wealdstone
maybe.*

TALES FROM THE VICARAGE

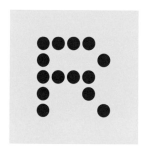

IS FOR...
RECORD BREAKERS

From the most goals in a game to the greatest ever
win, we salute the players, managers and results that
hold pride of place in the Watford record books.

TEAM

2nd
Highest First Division
finish, 1982/83

22
Most consecutive games
without defeat, 1996/97

8-0
Record league win
v Sunderland, 1982

11-0
Record league defeat
v Southampton, 1902

Wilf Rostron:
Wore the captain's
armband with
distinction in the
1980s glory years.

Paul Robinson:
Tough-tackling
full-back who wore
his heart on his
sleeve for his local
club and was
adored by fans.

MANAGERS

3
Managers who have won
promotion to the top
division *Graham Taylor,
Aidy Boothroyd, Slavisa
Jokanovic*

802
Most games as manager
Graham Taylor

5
Most promotions as
manager *Graham Taylor*

GOALS

186
Most goals
Luther Blissett

48
Most goals in a season
Cliff Holton, 1959/60

5
Most goals in a league match
Eddie Mummery, v Newport County, 1924

8
Goals in most consecutive games
Frank McPherson, 1928/29 and 1929/30

GAMES

503
Most appearances
Luther Blissett

280
Most league games in a row *Duncan Welbourne*

MISCELLANEOUS

44 years, 87 days
Oldest player
John Goodall, v Bradford Park Avenue, 1907

16 years, 125 days
Youngest player
Keith Mercer, v Tranmere Rovers, 1973

31
Most capped players
John Barnes, England
Kenny Jackett, Wales

34,099
Highest attendance
FA Cup fourth round, v Manchester United, 1969

George Reilly: Wrote his name into club folklore when he headed home against Plymouth to lead Watford to a first FA Cup final.

Sean Fulton:
Greatest ever
Watford FC
moment?
*The play-off final at
Wembley 1999.*

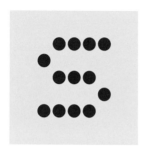

IS FOR...
SILVERWARE

From Herts County Cups in the 19th century to the Great Wall Cup on an end-of-season tour of China and the London Masters 6-a-side, Watford have won some interesting silverware over the years but, when it comes to major trophies, the club cabinet isn't exactly overflowing.

In addition to the play-off final trophies of 1999 and 2006, the Hornets have been crowned league champions five times in their history. The first came in the Southern League Second Division in 1900, and was followed by the First Division title in 1915 under the guidance of Harry Kent, who held the managerial reins for 16 years. On the penultimate day of the season, a goal from Fred Gregory sealed victory over Gillingham and top spot.

Les Simmons:
Legendary character and groundsman who spent more than 50 years at Vicarage Road.

The Hornets had to wait more than half a century before their next title in 1968/69. With barely any coins in the club coffers that decade, manager Ken Furphy had waved his magic wand to put together a team made up of free transfers and bargain signings. Future fan favourites Duncan Welbourne, Keith Eddy and Stewart Scullion were snapped up for less than £4,000 – combined – while Barry Endean, recruited from a pub team, top-scored that season with 18 league goals. Goalkeeper Mike Walker kept 23 clean sheets – still a club record – and played a huge part in

Ann Swanson:
The leader of Watford's work with the local community for many years.

TALES FROM THE VICARAGE

Watford edging out Swindon Town on goal difference to snatch the Third Division title.

Tommy Smith: Homegrown Hornet with the speed and skill to play up front or out wide, winning two player of the season awards.

In comparison, the race for the Fourth Division in 1977/78 was barely a contest. Making an instant impact under Graham Taylor, the Hornets romped to a record 30 wins to finish 11 points ahead of Southend, losing just once at home all season.

Taylor was at the helm again two decades later when Watford leapfrogged Bristol City on the final day of the 1997/98 Second Division season, thanks to Jason Lee's winner at Fulham. From Alec Chamberlain, Steve Palmer and Robert Page at the back, to Richard Johnson and Micah Hyde in the engine room, to Tommy Mooney up front, many of the title-winning team formed the nucleus of the side that would take on the might of Manchester United and co. in the Premier League 15 months later.

The Hornets romped to a record 30 wins to finish 11 points ahead of Southend, losing just once at home all season

TALES FROM THE VICARAGE

Mikey Bennett:
Whereabouts in
the Vicarage Road
stadium do you sit?
The Rookery End.

TALES FROM THE VICARAGE

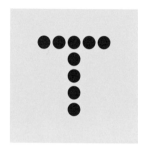

IS FOR...
TAYLOR

Such has been the impact of Graham Taylor's contribution to Watford that it feels remiss to devote just one letter of the alphabet to him. You could easily fill a whole A-Z with his achievements but, to Hornets fans, he will always be two letters – 'GT'.

" Taylor made it is his mission to unite Watford – the players, the club, the town. All in it together "

When Taylor took over as Watford manager in June 1977, after accepting an offer from chairman Elton John to leave Lincoln City and step down a division, few could have anticipated the radical transformation that would follow. Together, the pair put Watford on the football map as Taylor worked wonders to lead the club into uncharted territory.

From day one, he instilled discipline and a professional approach – among players, support staff and administration – and he also brought belief. Deploying wingers and big, athletic forwards, attack was at the forefront of his team's philosophy. The players ran themselves into the ground for their manager.

Les Taylor:
Player of the season in the team that won promotion to the First Division for the first time and captained Watford in the FA Cup final.

The results were astounding. In five seasons, Taylor took the Hornets from the Fourth to the First Division. In his sixth season came a second-placed finish behind Liverpool. In the seventh, a UEFA Cup run and an FA Cup final. Things like these weren't meant to happen at Watford.

After a decade, the in-demand manager moved on to Aston Villa, then the England job, but Vicarage Road would always be home. And on his return in 1997, he made the dreams of a new generation of Hornets come true. The Second Division title was followed by a play-off win and promotion to the Premier League a year later.

George Toone: Half-back who played in every one of Watford's first 159 Football League games.

And yet the miracles on the field are only one part of the story. Taylor made it is his mission to unite Watford – the players, the club, the town. All in it together. Through his tireless work in the local community and determination to create a family-friendly club, he gave the Hornets a new identity and brought them into everyone's lives.

Rod Thomas: Attacking player who became the youngest Hornet in the top division at just 17.

The outpouring of emotion after his sudden passing in January 2017, and the tributes from Watford and clubs up and down the country, spoke volumes of the man who was a treasured figure of English football. Nowhere more so than at Vicarage Road. Watford's greatest ever manager, and so much more.

TALES FROM THE VICARAGE

Ollie Gandy:
All-time favourite Watford FC player?
Tony Coton.

IS FOR...
UNEXPECTED

"This is the sort of result you dream about but don't really expect to happen." So spoke Graham Taylor in the aftermath of Watford's scarcely believable 7-1 League Cup second round defeat of Southampton in 1980.

Not only had the Second Division side destroyed the First Division high-flyers; they had overturned a 4-0 first-leg deficit at The Dell.

Over the years, Hornets fans have repeated Taylor's words time and again, as their team has defied expectations to produce the most unlikely results. Cup competitions have often been the scene of the biggest surprises, going back to 1960 when Watford belied its Fourth Division status to stun top-flight Birmingham on their way to the FA Cup fifth round. In 1970, the freshly crowned Third Division champions went even further, reaching the FA Cup last four after Barry Endean's strike knocked out Liverpool.

The list goes on and on: a 2-1 League Cup defeat of Manchester United at Old Trafford in 1978; UEFA Cup comebacks against Kaiserslautern and Levski Sofia in 1983; a 3-1 win at Highbury in the 1987 FA Cup quarter-final that still riles Arsenal fans today; knocking Eric Cantona's Leeds, the reigning league champions, out of the League Cup in 1992; reaching the 2003 FA Cup semi-final; reaching the 2005 League Cup semi-final; and beating Arsenal

Udinese:
Italian club also owned by the Pozzos and the source of many players, particularly in the 2012/13 season.

> **Victory over Tottenham in their first league appearance at White Hart Lane was a sign of things to come as the Hornets sprung shocks right up to the final day of the season**

in another FA Cup quarter-final in front of almost 60,000 fans at the Emirates Stadium in 2016.

Yet it was in the 1982/83 season – Watford's first ever in the top division – when they really made football's elite take notice, and take them seriously. Victory over Tottenham in their first league appearance at White Hart Lane was a sign of things to come as the Hornets sprung shocks right up to the final day of the season when a defeat of Liverpool guaranteed second place, and ruined manager Bob Paisley's farewell.

Liverpool were the victims again in 1999 when Tommy Mooney silenced Anfield in the Hornets' first foray into the Premier League, and the Merseysiders are among the Hornets' scalps, alongside Manchester United, Chelsea and Arsenal (twice), since their return to the top flight in 2015.

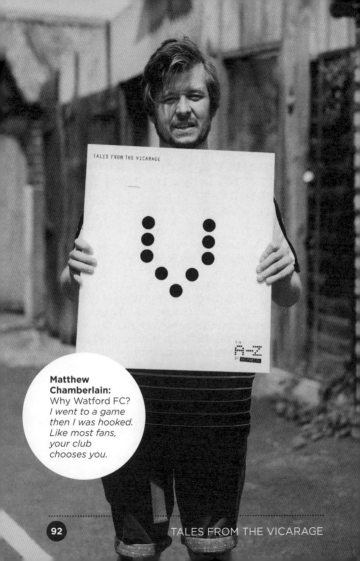

Matthew Chamberlain:
Why Watford FC? *I went to a game then I was hooked. Like most fans, your club chooses you.*

TALES FROM THE VICARAGE

IS FOR...
VICARAGE ROAD

Almost a century has passed since Watford upped roots from Cassio Road and moved home to Vicarage Road half a mile down the road. The newly built stadium first opened its gates to 8,618 fans on August 30 1922.

It may have been an inauspicious beginning – a goalless draw against Third Division South rivals Millwall – but the years that followed have seen a rich array of memorable matches and moments, including many famous nights under the lights.

Vicarage Road has also jointly served as the ground of Wealdstone FC (briefly) and Saracens (16 years), hosted greyhound racing and horse shows, been sold, been bought back again, and undergone plenty of facelifts on its way to becoming the all-seater stadium with a capacity of more than 23,000 that the Hornets call home today.

Back in 1922, there were two covered stands – the Union Stand, brought over from Cassio Road, and the Main Stand – plus terraces. The Union Stand became the Shrodells Stand in the 1930s, then the two-tiered Rous Stand in 1986, before being renamed the Graham Taylor Stand in 2014. That was the same year that the Main Stand, home of the pioneering family enclosure at the end of the 1970s, was reborn as the

....

" Situated at the south of the stadium, the Rookery End is very much the heart and soul of Vicarage Road, and home to the biggest – and loudest – collection of Watford fans "

....

Matej Vydra:
Lightning-quick
forward whose
goals almost
brought Premier
League promotion
in 2013.

Sir Elton John Stand, after being closed for many years. The lyrics from Elton's hit *Your Song* are written across the back wall of the stand from where he used to watch his beloved Hornets as a child.

It wasn't until the mid-1990s that the terraces behind both goals were developed from standing to seating, helped by funds raised from the sales of strike partners Paul Furlong and Bruce Dyer. In 1993, the terrace at the north of the ground – known for its iconic electronic scoreboard with jumping figures in the 1980s – became the Vicarage Road Stand. It is now home to Watford's family section and the away fans.

Last but by no means least, the Rookery Stand was built in 1995. Situated at the south of the stadium, the Rookery End is very much the heart and soul of Vicarage Road, and home to the biggest – and loudest – collection of Watford fans, including the 1881 Movement singing section.

TALES FROM THE VICARAGE

Jon Moonie:
Whereabouts in
the Vicarage Road
stadium do you sit?
The Rookery End.

TALES FROM THE VICARAGE

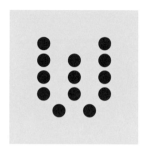

IS FOR...
WEMBLEY

For a venue that conjures up so many magical memories, the home of football has not always been kind to Watford. In fact, as of the April 2018 Premier League fixture against Tottenham, the Hornets have ended up on the losing side on four out of five visits to Wembley.

⁖ **As the tears flowed from the fans, and Elton John, at the final whistle, Watford had won a place in the nation's hearts** ⁖

And yet the national stadium has provided the scene for some of the greatest occasions in the club's history, and none bigger than the 1984 FA Cup final.

The Hornets' fairytale road to Wembley began with a 4-3 replay win against rivals Luton. Victories over Charlton, Brighton and Birmingham were followed by a 1-0 semi-final defeat of Plymouth at Villa Park.

Duncan Welbourne: Frighteningly fit wide man who played an astonishing 280 league games in a row.

And so on May 19 1984 a suited Graham Taylor led his team onto the Wembley turf, and into the global spotlight, for the FA Cup final against Everton and a first appearance at a stadium dazzling in a sea of yellow shirts. Graeme Sharp gave Everton the lead, chances came and went for Les Taylor, John Barnes and Maurice Johnston, before the controversial moment that still rankles with Hornets fans today – when Andy Gray headed the ball out of goalkeeper Steve Sherwood's hands and into the net.

As the tears flowed from the fans, and Elton John, at the final whistle, Watford had won a place in the nation's hearts.

There was further Wembley woe in the 2013 play-off final and 2016 FA Cup semi-final, both times at the hands of Crystal Palace, but it was a different story at the home of football in the 1999 play-off final.

Just one year on from winning the Second Division title, only Bolton Wanderers stood between the Hornets and a first ever trip to the Premier League.

Skilly Williams: Legendary goalkeeper who played more than 300 games either side of serving in World War One.

After a tight start, it took a moment of magic from Nick Wright to break the deadlock, his perfectly flighted overhead kick nestling into the top corner.

The result was settled when Allan Smart smashed home a second in the 89th minute, sending the yellow half of Wembley into raptures as Taylor celebrated a fifth promotion with the Hornets.

Johnny Williams: Member of the Third Division title team who racked up 400-plus appearances over a decade.

THE A-Z OF WATFORD FC

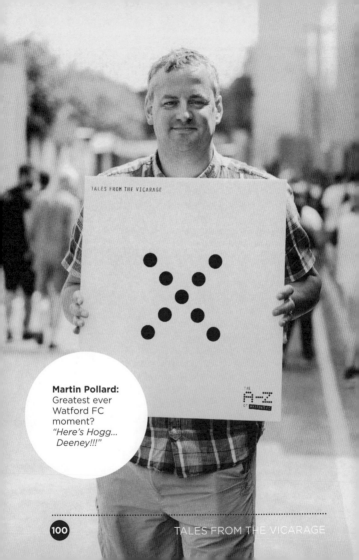

TALES FROM THE VICARAGE

Martin Pollard:
Greatest ever Watford FC moment?
*"Here's Hogg...
Deeney!!!"*

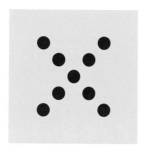

IS FOR...
X-FACTOR

When Stewart Scullion unleashed a glorious 25-yard drive to open the scoring against Manchester United in the fourth round of the FA Cup in 1969, the reigning European champions couldn't believe what they had just seen.

> **To many supporters, 'Cally' will always be the best Hornet never to have been capped by England.**

Not so Watford fans, though, who had witnessed many similar moments of magic in the Third Division and were well aware of the Scottish winger's talents. A wizardry dribbler with superb skills, Scullion's name sits prominently among Watford players who have been blessed with the X-factor, that special ability to produce something so breathtaking it makes the stadium gasp – be it conjuring a goal out of nothing or playing a pass no one else could see.

Nigel Callaghan carried on Scullion's tradition of terrorising hapless full-backs in the 1980s. With John Barnes flying down the left flank, 'Cally' was the perfect foil on the right, time and again putting pinpoint crosses on Ross Jenkins's head. To many supporters, he will always be the best Hornet never to have been capped by England.

The following decade, it was Craig Ramage who illuminated Vicarage Road during some dark times in the mid-1990s. The midfielder's skills and swagger

were a joy to behold; he memorably came to the fore at the end of the 1995/96 season, scoring a hat-trick in a 6-3 thrashing of Grimsby and pulling the strings as Watford – seemingly dead and buried – almost pulled off the greatest of escapes from relegation.

Others who have shown that special something in the yellow, red and black include – but are by no means limited to – Richard Johnson, the Australian midfielder and master of the stunning long-range goal; Gifton Noel-Williams, the Hornets' youngest ever goalscorer; Ashley Young, the creative spirit of Aidy Boothroyd's promotion-winning side; and Almen Abdi and Fernando Forestieri, who produced touches of genius that their manager Gianfranco Zola would have been proud of in his pomp.

For a different kind of X-factor, look no further than Steve Palmer, the ultimate utility who wore every shirt from one to 14 in the 1997/98 season – with a little help from Graham Taylor. In the penultimate game, the manager started Palmer in goal and keeper Alec Chamberlain in defence before the Hornets booted the ball out for a throw-in and the players swapped back to their more comfortable positions.

TALES FROM THE VICARAGE

John Parslow:
First Watford
FC game?
*April 1977, Watford
2-0 v Huddersfield.
Mike Keen's last
match, then
came GT.*

IS FOR...
YELLOWS

Jim Bonser is the man whom Hornets fans have to thank for bringing yellow into Watford's life. Or at least a touch of gold.

"In 1976, the year that Elton John took over the club, the gold morphed into yellow, and the Golden Boys became the Yellow Army"

Following the club's demotion to the Fourth Division in 1958 as part of the restructuring of the Football League, the new chairman was keen to introduce some fairly radical changes and move away from the past. And so it was that Watford changed their colours to gold and black for the 1959/60 season. Such was the state of the club's finances at the time – or perhaps the desperation to replace the blue-and-white colours of the past three decades – that the Watford Supporters Club even offered to pay for the kit.

"You don't get cramp at this club": Immortal line from Graham Taylor to one of his players in his first season in charge.

With the new colours came a new name – the Hornets – and an instant upturn in form, which brought promotion to the Third Division and an unlikely run to the fifth round of the FA Cup. Then in 1976, the year that Elton John took over the club, the gold morphed into yellow, and the Golden Boys became the Yellow Army. Watford were kitted out in yellow shirts, black shorts and black socks – with a splash of red and yellow – and the yellow identity that we're so familiar with today was born.

Once again, the change in colours led to a change in fortunes, as the Hornets embarked on their incredible run through the divisions. And in a further sign of that success, the club shirt was sponsored for the first time in the 1982/83 season, by Iveco. Since then, many more sponsors have come and gone – from Blaupunkt, Beko and Bet138, to Total and Toshiba, to Phones4U, Football Manager and FxPro.

Every fan has a favourite, be it the Solvite-sponsored shirt with the red-and-black horizontal stripe or the CTX 1999 play-off final strip, complete with red shoulder pads. And the age-old debate about whether the Hornets should wear red or black shorts rumbles on every season.

Ashley Young: Graduate from the youth academy who starred in the Championship and Premier League.

Whatever the choice, there are few more vibrant sights in football than the Vicarage Road stands packed to the rafters with yellow shirts or, on those most special of occasions, one half of Wembley or the Millennium Stadium radiating with yellow.

TALES FROM THE VICARAGE

Philip Lam:
Why Watford FC?
*I moved here and
just enjoyed the
town and the
heritage.*

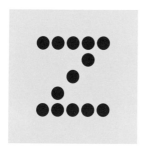

IS FOR...
Z-CARS

Of all the different experiences encountered on a matchday at Vicarage Road, there is one moment that never changes. In the final minutes before kick-off as the players emerge from the tunnel, a very familiar tune blasts through the PA system.

The music from the TV programme *Z-Cars* was first played at a home match more than half a century ago, and arouses a wide range of emotions in Watford fans – be it the spine-tingling anticipation of the 90 minutes that lie ahead or the sudden realisation that it's time to run to your seat!

But what links Watford and a 1960s Lancashire-based police drama series? The answer lies in a manager who loved the TV show and clearly believed in omens.

After Watford lost at home to Peterborough on October 5 1963, Bill McGarry decided something had to change. Ten days later, when the Hornets faced Crystal Palace, the manager arranged for the *Z-Cars* theme tune to be played before kick-off as the teams walked on to the pitch. Watford won 3-1. The following Saturday, the same music blared out before a 2-0 victory over old rivals Luton.

A tradition was born, and *Z-Cars* became McGarry's lucky charm. With the tune being played at the start of every home match for the rest of the season, Watford didn't lose another league game at Vicarage Road and, come season's end, had climbed to third in the Third Division just a couple of points off promotion; at the time, it was the club's highest ever final position in the Football League. Incredibly, the unbeaten home run lasted more than a year and only came to an end on December 19 1964, by which point Ken Furphy was in charge and *Z-Cars* was firmly in the club's DNA.

Gianfranco Zola: Hugely popular Italian manager who served up thrilling football and a run to the Championship play-off final.

Whisper it quietly, but Everton also play the same pre-match tune at Goodison Park, and started doing so a year earlier than Watford. However – just like the 1984 FA Cup final – let's forget about that.

❝ **With the tune being played at the start of every home match for the rest of the season, Watford didn't lose another league game at Vicarage Road** ❞

Other Tales From The Vicarage titles

TALES FROM THE
VICARAGE
THE INTERVIEWS
BY LIONEL BIRNIE
& ADAM LEVENTHAL

TALES FROM THE VICARAGE

CAPTAINS

VOLUME 7 BY MIKE WALTERS

TALES FROM THE VICARAGE
ROCKET
MEN
VOLUME 6 BY OLIVER PHILLIPS AND MIKE WALTERS

FEATURING
BLISSETT
BOLTON
JENKINS
SHERWOOD

FOREWORD BY
JOHN BARNES

Volumes 1-7
available via
www.talesfrom.com

Colin Mace:
First Watford
FC game?
*FA Cup fourth
round 1969 at
Old Trafford.*

Front cover:
Charlie Knight:
Greatest ever Watford FC moment?
Being mascot vs Stoke City 2 years ago.

Back cover:
Linda Anderson
Why Watford FC?
*It's a family club with community values at its heart,
and that is priceless.*